The Orchard Book

of **Funny Poems**

The Orchard Book of Nursery Rhymes

Faith Jaques

The Orchard Book of Nursery Stories

Sophie Windham

The Orchard Book of Fairy Tales

Retold by Rose Impey
Illustrated by Ian Beck

The Orchard Book of Greek Myths

Retold by Geraldine McCaughrean
Illustrated by Emma Chichester Clark

The Orchard Book of Magical Tales

Retold by Margaret Mayo
Illustrated by Jane Ray

The Orchard Book of Poems

Compiled by Adrian Mitchell

The Orchard Book

of **Funny Poems**

Compiled by

WENDY COPE

Illustrated by

AMANDA VESEY

ORCHARD BOOKS

For Pauline
A.V.

In memory of Margaret Arnold (1900 – 1991),
a good friend to every child she knew.

My thanks to the following for their advice and assistance: the staff of the
Saison Poetry Library, especially Dolores Conway, the children's librarian; Ian
Willison and John Barr of the British Library; Morag Styles.
Wendy Cope

ORCHARD BOOKS
96 Leonard Street, London EC2A 4RH
Orchard Books Australia
14 Mars Road, Lane Cove, NSW 2066
ISBN 1 85213 395 3 (hardback)
ISBN 1 86039 101 X (paperback)
First published in Great Britain 1993
First paperback publication 1996
Text © Wendy Cope 1993
Illustrations © Amanda Vesey 1993
The right of Wendy Cope to be identified as the compiler
and Amanda Vesey as the illustrator of this work has been
asserted by them in accordance with the Copyright,
Designs and Patents Act, 1988.
A CIP catalogue record for this book is available from the British Library.
Printed in Singapore

Contents

Easy Money

Guess how old I am?
I bet you can't.
I bet you.
Go on guess.
Have a guess.

Wrong!
Have another.

Wrong!
Have another.

Wrong again!
Do you give in?

Seven years four months two weeks
five days three hours fifteen
minutes forty-eight seconds!
That's 20p you owe me.

Roger McGough

Telling

One, two, three, four,
Telling Miss that Gary swore.
Five, six, seven, eight,
Now I haven't got a mate.

Wendy Cope

A Quick Way of Counting to 100

1,2,
skip a few,
99, 100

Anon

1 × 2 is 2

1 × 2 is 2
2 × 2 are 4
3 × 2 are 9
4 × 2 are 17
5 × 2 are 26
6 × 2 are 39
7 × 2 are 148
8 × 2 are 2,204
9 × 2 are 330,916
10 × 2 are 999,999
11 × 2 are 5,222,506½
12 × 2 are 135,926,201

and if anyone says it isn't
meet me in the playground
tomorrow at high noon,
and don't be late! . . .

Paul Johnson

As I was Going to St Ives

As I was going to St Ives,
I met a man with seven wives;
Every wife had seven sacks;
Every sack had seven cats;
Every cat had seven kits.
Kits, cats, sacks, and wives –
How many were going to St Ives?

Anon

Answer: One. The others
were coming from St Ives.

Three Riddled Riddles

1

I have nine legs.
I carry an umbrella.
I live in a box
at the bottom of a ship.
At night
I play the trombone.

What am I?

Answer: I've forgotten.

2

You see me at dawn
with the clouds in my hair.
I run like a horse
and sing like a nightingale.
I collect stamps
and coconuts.

What am I?

Answer: I'm not sure.

3

I taste like a grapefruit.
I swim like a chair.
I hang on the trees
and people tap my face,
rake my soil
and tell me jokes.

What am I?

Answer: I've really no idea.

Martyn Wiley and Ian McMillan

Cottleston Pie

Cottleston, Cottleston, Cottleston Pie,
A fly can't bird, but a bird can fly.
Ask me a riddle and I reply:
"Cottleston, Cottleston, Cottleston Pie."

Cottleston, Cottleston, Cottleston Pie,
A fish can't whistle and neither can I.
Ask me a riddle and I reply:
"Cottleston, Cottleston, Cottleston Pie."

Cottleston, Cottleston, Cottleston Pie,
Why does a chicken, I don't know why.
Ask me a riddle and I reply:
"Cottleston, Cottleston, Cottleston Pie."

A.A. Milne

Here Is the Nose that Smelled Something Sweet

Here is the Nose that smelled something sweet
And led the search for a bite to eat

Here are the Feet that followed the Nose
Around the kitchen on ten Tiptoes

Here are the Eyes that looked high and low
Till they spotted six pans sitting all in a row

Here are the Arms that reached up high
To bring down a fresh-baked blueberry pie

Here is the Mouth that opened up wide
Here are the Hands that put pie inside

Here is the Tongue that licked the tin
And lapped up the juice running down the Chin

Here is the Stomach that growled for more
Here are the Legs that ran for the door

Here are the Ears that heard a whack
Here is the Bottom that felt a smack!

Clyde Watson

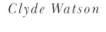

If You're No Good at Cooking

If you're no good at cooking,
Can't fry or bake,

Here's something you
Can always make. Take

Three very ordinary
Slices of bread:

Stack the second
On the first one's head.

Stack the third
On top of that.

There! Your three slices
Lying pat.

So what have you got?
A BREAD SANDWICH,

That's what!
Why not?

Kit Wright

Christine Crump

Christine Crump is crunching crisps:
Cheese and onion, cheese and onion.
Christine Crump has crunched them.

Christine Crump is crunching crisps:
Smoky bacon, smoky bacon,
Cheese and onion, cheese and onion.
Christine Crump has crunched them.

Christine Crump is crunching crisps:
Ready salted, ready salted,
Smoky bacon, smoky bacon,
Cheese and onion, cheese and onion.
Christine Crump has crunched them.

Christine Crump is crunching crisps:
Curry flavour, curry flavour,
Ready salted, ready salted,
Smoky bacon, smoky bacon,
Cheese and onion, cheese and onion.
Christine Crump has crunched them.

Christine Crump is crunching crisps:
Salt and vinegar, salt and vinegar,
Curry flavour, curry flavour,
Ready salted, ready salted,
Smoky bacon, smoky bacon,
Cheese and onion, cheese and onion.
Christine Crump has crunched them.

Christine Crump is feeling sick . . .
Poor old Christine, poor old Christine,
She has indigestion.

Colin West

Through the Teeth

Through the teeth
And past the gums
Look out stomach,
Here it comes!

Anon

Maa-a-a

Maa-a-a?
Yes, my dear.
Maaaaa-a-a?
Yes, my dear.
Maa-aa, do plums have legs?
No, my dear.
Then danged if I ain't ate a snoddywig!

Anon

Chips

They don't have any stones
They don't have any pips
They don't have any bones
That's why I like chips.

Julie Holder

Puddin' Song

Oh, who would be a puddin',
   A puddin' in a pot,
A puddin' which is stood on
   A fire which is hot?
Oh sad indeed the lot
Of puddin's in a pot.

I wouldn't be a puddin'
   If I could be a bird,
If I could be a wooden
   Doll, I would'n' say a word.
Yes, I have often heard
It's grand to be a bird.

But as I am a puddin',
   A puddin' in a pot,
I hope you get the stomachache
   For eatin' me a lot.
I hope you get it hot,
You puddin'-eatin' lot!

Norman Lindsay

My Brother's on the Floor

My brother's on the floor roaring
my brother's on the floor roaring
why is my brother on the floor roaring?
My brother is on the floor roaring
because he's supposed to finish his beans
before he has his pudding.

But he doesn't want to finish his beans
before he has his pudding

he says he wants his pudding
NOW.

But they won't let him

so now my brother is . . . on the floor roaring.

They're saying
I give you one more chance to finish those beans
or you don't go to Tony's
but he's not listening because . . .
he's on the floor roaring.

20

He's getting told off
I'm not
I've eaten my beans.

Do you know what I'm doing now?
I'm eating my pudding
and . . . he's on the floor roaring.

If he wasn't . . . on the floor roaring
he'd see me eating my pudding
and if he looked really close
he might see a little tiny smile
just at the corner of my mouth.
But he's not looking . . .
he's on the floor roaring.

The pudding is OK
it's not wonderful
not wonderful enough
to be sitting on the floor and roaring about
unless you're my brother.

Michael Rosen

Brother

I had a little brother
And I brought him to my mother
And I said I want another
Little brother for a change.
But she said don't be a bother
So I took him to my father
And I said this little bother
Of a brother's very strange.

But he said one little brother
Is exactly like another
And every little brother
Misbehaves a bit he said.
So I took the little bother
From my mother and my father
And I put the little bother
Of a brother back to bed.

Mary Ann Hobermann

Mum is Having a Baby

Mum is having a baby!
I'm shocked! I'm all at sea!
What's she want another one for:
WHAT'S THE MATTER WITH ME?

Colin McNaughton

Willie Built a Guillotine

Willie built a guillotine,
Tried it out on sister Jean.
Said Mother as she got the mop:
"These messy games have got to stop!"

William E. Engel

An Accident Happened to My Brother Jim

An accident happened to my brother Jim
When somebody threw a tomato at him –
Tomatoes are juicy and don't hurt the skin,
But this one was specially packed in a tin.

Anon

Adventures of Isabel

Isabel met an enormous bear,
Isabel, Isabel, didn't care;
The bear was hungry, the bear was ravenous,
The bear's big mouth was cruel and cavernous.
The bear said, "Isabel, glad to meet you,
How do, Isabel, now I'll eat you!"
Isabel, Isabel, didn't worry,
Isabel didn't scream or scurry.
She washed her hands and she straightened her hair up
Then Isabel quietly ate the bear up.

Once in a night as black as pitch
Isabel met a wicked old witch.
The witch's face was cross and wrinkled,
The witch's gums with teeth were sprinkled.
"Ho ho, Isabel!" the old witch crowed,
"I'll turn you into an ugly toad!"
Isabel, Isabel, didn't worry,
Isabel didn't scream or scurry,
She showed no rage and she showed no rancour,
But she turned the witch into milk and drank her.

Isabel met a hideous giant,
Isabel continued self-reliant.
The giant was hairy, the giant was horrid,
He had one eye in the middle of his forehead.
"Good morning, Isabel," the giant said,
"I'll grind your bones to make my bread."
Isabel, Isabel, didn't worry,
Isabel didn't scream or scurry.
She nibbled the zwieback that she always fed off,
And when it was gone, she cut the giant's head off.

Isabel met a troublesome doctor,
He punched and he poked till he really shocked her.
The doctor's talk was of coughs and chills
And the doctor's satchel bulged with pills.
The doctor said unto Isabel,
"Swallow this, it will make you well."
Isabel, Isabel, didn't worry,
Isabel didn't scream or scurry.
She took those pills from the pill concoctor,
And Isabel calmly cured the doctor.

Isabel once was asleep in bed
When a horrible dream crawled into her head.
It was worse than a dinosaur, worse than a shark,
Worse than an octopus oozing in the dark.
"Boo!" said the dream, with a dreadful grin,
"I'm going to scare you out of your skin!"
Isabel, Isabel, didn't worry,
Isabel didn't scream or scurry,
Isabel had a cleverer scheme;
She just woke up and fooled that dream.

Whenever you meet a bugaboo
Remember what Isabel used to do.
Don't scream when the bugaboo says "Boo!"
Just look it in the eye and say, "Boo to you!"
That's how to banish a bugaboo;
Isabel did it and so can you!
Boooooo to you.

Ogden Nash

My Cousin Melda

My Cousin Melda
she don't make fun
she ain't afraid of anyone
even mosquitoes
when they bite her
she does bite them back
and say
"Now tell me – HOW YOU LIKE THAT?"

Grace Nichols

Deborah Delora

Deborah Delora, she liked a bit of fun –
She went to the baker's and she bought a penny bun,
Dipped the bun in treacle and threw it at her teacher –
Deborah Delora! What a wicked creature!

Anon

L

I shan't forget that little villain, L,
Who plagued me for a year in Class 4C.
She used to take delight in raising hell.

Her name I won't reveal – it's just as well
To hide the dreadful child's identity.
I shan't forget that little villain, L.

The fire-alarm went off – she rang the bell
After she locked me in the lavatory.
She used to take delight in raising hell.

The day we went pond-dipping, in she fell!
She couldn't swim, though I could, luckily.
I shan't forget that little villain, L.

She let the gerbils out – they ran pell-mell.
Miss Pringle ended up in Casualty.
She used to take delight in raising hell.

Although she was a problem, truth to tell,
I missed her when she ran away to sea.
I shan't forget that little villain, L.
She used to take delight in raising hell.

Sue Cowling

here Was a Naughty Boy

. . . There was a naughty Boy,
  And a naughty Boy was he,
He ran away to Scotland
  The people for to see –
    There he found
    That the ground
    Was as hard,
    That a yard
    Was as long,
    That a song
    Was as merry,
    That a cherry
    Was as red –
    That lead
    Was as weighty,
    That fourscore
    Was as eighty,
    That a door
    Was as wooden
    As in England –
So he stood in his shoes
  And he wondered,
    He wondered,
He stood in his shoes
  And he wondered.

John Keats

Into the Mixer

Into the mixer he went,
    the nosy boy,
into the mess of wet cement,
    round and round
    with a glugging sound
and a boyish screamed complaint.

Out of the mixer he came,
    the concrete boy,
onto the road made of the same
    quick-setting stuff.
    He looked rough
and he'd only himself to blame.

Matthew Sweeney

The Human Siren

Tim, Tim, the human siren,
LOUDEST boy in town.
Tim, Tim, the human siren,
Never lets you down.

Tim, Tim, the human siren,
When he's not at play,
We rent him to the fire brigade
At fifteen pounds a day.

Colin McNaughton

I Din Do Nuttin

I din do nuttin
I din do nuttin
I din do nuttin
All I did
was throw Granny pin
in the rubbish bin.

I din do nuttin
I din do nuttin
I din do nuttin
All I did
was mix paint in
Mammy biscuit tin.

I din do nuttin
I din do nuttin.

John Agard

Why Did the Children

"Why did the children
put beans in their ears
when the one thing we told the children
they must not do
was put beans in their ears?"

"Why did the children
pour molasses on the cat
when the one thing we told the children
they must not do
was pour molasses on the cat?"

Carl Sandburg

Endless Chant

"Who put the overalls in Mrs Murphy's chowder?"
Nobody answered, so she said it all the louder:
"Who put the overalls in Mrs Murphy's chowder?"
Nobody answered, so she said it all the louder:
"Who put the overalls in Mrs Murphy's chowder?"
Nobody answered, so she said it all the louder:
"Who put the overalls in Mrs Murphy's chowder?"
Nobody answered, so she said it all the louder:
"Who put the overalls in Mrs Murphy's chowder?"
Nobody answered, so she said it all the louder:
"Who put the overalls in Mrs Murphy's chowder?"
Nobody answered, so she said it all the louder:
"Who put the overalls in Mrs Murphy's chowder?"
Nobody answered, so she said it all the louder:
"Who put the overalls in Mrs Murphy's chowder?"
Nobody answered, so she said it all the louder:
"Who put the overalls in Mrs Murphy's chowder?"
Nobody answered, so she said it all the louder:
"Who put the overalls in Mrs Murphy's chowder?"
Nobody answered, so she said it all the louder:
"Who put the overalls in Mrs Murphy's chowder?"
Nobody answered, so she said it all the louder:
"Who put the overalls in Mrs Murphy's chowder?"

Nobody answered, so she said it all the louder:
"Who put the overalls in Mrs Murphy's chowder?"
Nobody answered, so she said it all the louder:
"Who put the overalls in Mrs Murphy's chowder?"
Nobody answered, so she said it all the louder:
"Who put the overalls in Mrs Murphy's chowder?"
Nobody answered, so she said it all the louder:
"Who put the overalls in Mrs Murphy's chowder?"
Nobody answered, so she said it all the louder:
"Who put the overalls in Mrs Murphy's chowder?"
Nobody answered, so she said it all the louder:
"Who put the overalls in Mrs Murphy's chowder?"
Nobody answered, so she said it all the louder:
"Who put the overalls in Mrs Murphy's chowder?"
Nobody answered, so she said it all the louder:
"Who put the overalls in Mrs Murphy's chowder?"
Nobody answered, so she said it all the louder:
"Who put the overalls in Mrs Murphy's chowder?"
Nobody answered, so she said it all the louder:
"Who put the overalls in Mrs Murphy's chowder?"
Nobody answered, so she said it all the louder:
"Who put the overalls in Mrs Murphy's chowder?"

Anon

Monday's Child is Red and Spotty

Monday's child is red and spotty,
Tuesday's child won't use the potty.
Wednesday's child won't go to bed,
Thursday's child will not be fed.
Friday's child breaks all his toys,
Saturday's child makes an awful noise.
And the child that's born on the seventh day
Is a pain in the neck like the rest, OK!

Colin McNaughton

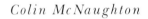

I'm in a Rotten Mood

I'm in a rotten mood today,
a really rotten mood today,
I'm feeling cross,
I'm feeling mean,
I'm jumpy as a jumping bean,
I have an awful attitude –
I'M IN A ROTTEN MOOD!

I'm in a rotten mood today,
a really rotten mood today,
I'm in a snit,
I'm in a stew,
there's nothing that I care to do
but sit all by myself and brood –
I'M IN A ROTTEN MOOD!

I'm in a rotten mood today,
a really rotten mood today,
you'd better stay away from me,
I'm just a lump of misery,
I'm feeling absolutely rude –
I'M IN A ROTTEN MOOD!

Jack Prelutsky

The Song of a Mole

All I did this afternoon was
Dig, dig, dig,
And all I'll do tomorrow will be
Dig, dig, dig,
And yesterday from dusk till dawn
I dug, dug, dug.
I sometimes think I'd rather be
A slug, slug, slug.

Richard Edwards

Sometime the Cow Kick your Head

Sometime the cow kick your head
Sometime she just moo

Even the cow don't know
What she going to do

Until she look at you
Knocked out upon the ground

And she say, "Woo
My leg do that to him"

Andrew J. Grossman

Not a Word

They walked the lane together,
The sky was dotted with stars.
They reached the rails together,
He lifted up the bars.
She neither smiled nor thanked him,
Because she knew not how,
For he was only the farmer's boy
And she was the Jersey cow!

Anon

Commissariat Camels

We haven't a camelty tune of our own
To help us trollop along,
But every neck is a hair-trombone
(*Rtt-ta-ta-ta*! is a hair-trombone!)
And this is our marching-song:
Can't! Don't! Shan't! Won't!
Pass it along the line!
Somebody's pack has slid from his back,
'Wish it were only mine!
Somebody's load has tipped off in the road –
Cheer for a halt and a row!
Urr! Yarrh! Grr! Arrh!
Somebody's catching it now!

Rudyard Kipling

Giraffes Don't Huff

Giraffes don't huff or hoot or howl
They never grump, they never growl
They never roar, they never riot,
They eat green leaves
And just keep quiet.

Karla Kuskin

The Tree Frog

The tree frog
Creaks and croaks and croaks
And says, "Dee deep"
On elms and oaks,
"Dee deep," he says
And stops, till when
It's time to say
"Dee deep" again.

John Travers Moore

What a Wonderful Bird the Frog Are

What a wonderful bird the frog are:–
When he sit, he stand almost;
When he hop, he fly almost.
He ain't got no sense hardly;
He ain't got no tail either,
When he sit, he sit on what he ain't got – almost.

Anon

The Dobermann Dog, O the Dobermann Dog

The Dobermann dog, O the Dobermann dog,
O why did they buy me the Dobermann dog?
he is bigger than I am
by more than a half
and so clumsy at play
it would make a cat laugh –
he sprawls and he falls
over tables and chairs
and goes over his nose when he
stalks down the stairs.
He's the colour of seedcake
mixed with old tar
and he never knows rightly
where his feet are –
he growls in a fashion
to bully all Britain
but it doesn't so much as
frighten my kitten.
On the table at tea-time
he rests his big jaw
and rolls his gentle eyes
for one crumb more.

How often he tumbles me
on the green lawn
then he licks me and stands
looking rather forlorn
like a cockadoo waiting the
sun in the morn.
I call him my Dobe
O my Dobermann dog
my Obermann Dobermann
yes, my Octobermann
Obermann Dobermann Dog.

George Barker

Literalist

R U A B I C?
O O U R A B!

John Fandel

Question

Do you love me
Or do you not?
You told me once
But I forgot.

Anon

It's Hard to Lose Your Lover

It's hard to lose your lover
When your heart is full of hope
But it's worse to lose your towel
When your eyes are full of soap.

Anon

When you Get Married

When you get married,
And your husband gets cross,
Just pick up the broom
And ask who's boss.

Anon

Friendship

I've discovered a way to stay friends for ever
There's really nothing to it.
I simply tell you what to do
And you do it!

Shel Silverstein

The Leader

I wanna be the leader
I wanna be the leader
Can I be the leader?
Can I? Can I?
Promise? Promise?
Yippee, I'm the leader
I'm the leader

OK what shall we do?

Roger McGough

Mr Skinner

Orville Skinner
(kite-string spinner)
never stopped
to eat his dinner,
for he found it
too exciting
and rewarding
to go kiting.

Flying kites,
he used to sing:
"I'm a spinner
on a string!"
When they warned him:
"Mister Skinner,
capable
but high-strung spinner,
it may take you
to Brazil,"
Skinner cried:
"I hope it will!"

N. M. Bodecker

here Was an Old Woman

There was an old woman of Chester-le-Street
Who chased a policeman all over his beat.

She shattered his helmet and tattered his clothes
And knocked his new spectacles clean off his nose.

"I'm afraid," said the Judge, "I must make it quite clear
You can't get away with that sort of thing here."

"I can and I will," the old woman she said,
"And I don't give a fig for your water and bread.

"I don't give a hoot for your cold prison cell,
And your bolts and your bars and your handcuffs as well.

"I've never been one to do just as I'm bid.
You can put me in jail for a year!"
                                    So they did.

Charles Causley

The Burglar

When the burglar went out
to burgle a house

When the burglar pulled on
his black polo-neck,
his beret, his Reeboks

When the burglar rattled
his skeleton keys,
checked he had his street-map,
said goodbye to his budgie

When the burglar shouldered
an empty bag, big enough
to take as much swag
as the burglar could carry

When the burglar waited
for the bus

When the burglar stood
at the bottom of the street
where the house he'd picked
to burgle was

When the burglar burgled
he didn't know
that another burglar
was inside *his* house

And only the budgie would see

Matthew Sweeney

The Village Burglar

Under the spreading gooseberry bush
   The village burglar lies;
The burglar is a hairy man
   With whiskers round his eyes.

He goes to church on Sundays;
   He hears the Parson shout;
He puts a penny in the plate
   And takes a shilling out.

Anon

Bad Sir Brian Botany

Sir Brian had a battleaxe with great big knobs on;
  He went among the villagers and blipped them on
    the head.
On Wednesday and on Saturday, but mostly on the
    latter day,
  He called at all the cottages, and this is what he said:
    "I am Sir Brian!" (*ting-ling*)
    "I am Sir Brian!" (*rat-tat*)
    "I am Sir Brian, as bold as a lion –
      Take *that!* – and *that!* – and *that!*"

Sir Brian had a pair of boots with great big spurs o
  A fighting pair of which he was particularly fond
On Tuesday and on Friday, just to make the street l
    tidy,
  He'd collect the passing villagers and kick them i
    the pond.
    "I am Sir Brian!" (*sper-lash!*)
    "I am Sir Brian!" (*sper-lash!*)
    "I am Sir Brian, as bold as a lion –
      Is anyone else for a wash?"

Sir Brian woke one morning, and he couldn't find his
    battleaxe;
  He walked into the village in his second pair of
    boots.
He had gone a hundred paces, when the street was full
    of faces,
  And the villagers were round him with ironical
    salutes.

"You are Sir Brian? Indeed!
  You are Sir Brian? Dear, dear!
You are Sir Brian, as bold as a lion?
  Delighted to meet you here!"

Sir Brian went a journey, and he found a lot of duck-
      weed:
    They pulled him out and dried him, and they blipped
      him on the head.
  They took him by the breeches, and they hurled him
      into ditches,
    And they pushed him under waterfalls, and this is
      what they said:
        "You are Sir Brian – don't laugh,
          You are Sir Brian – don't cry;
        You are Sir Brian, as bold as a lion –
          Sir Brian, the lion, good-bye!"

Sir Brian struggled home again, and chopped up his
    battleaxe,
  Sir Brian took his fighting boots, and threw them in
    the fire.
He is quite a different person now he hasn't got his
    spurs on,
  And he goes about the village as B. Botany, Esquire.

  "I am Sir Brian? Oh, *no!*
    I am Sir Brian? Who's he?
  I haven't got any title, I'm Botany –
    Plain Mr Botany (B)."

A. A. Milne

A Tragic Story

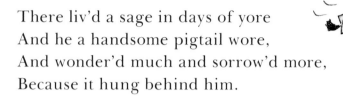

There liv'd a sage in days of yore
And he a handsome pigtail wore,
And wonder'd much and sorrow'd more,
Because it hung behind him.

He mus'd upon this curious case,
And swore he'd change the pigtail's place,
And have it hanging at his face,
Not dangling there behind him.

Says he, "The mystery I've found –
I'll turn me round."
He turned him round,
But still it hung behind him.

Then round and round, and out and in,
All day the puzzled sage did spin;
In vain – it matter'd not a pin,
The pigtail hung behind him.

And right and left, and round about,
And up and down, and in and out
He turn'd, but still the pigtail stout
Hung steadily behind him.

And though his efforts never slack,
And though he twist, and twirl, and tack,
Alas! still faithful to his back,
The pigtail hangs behind him.

William Makepeace Thackeray

A Tone-Deaf Old Person of Tring

A tone-deaf old person of Tring,
When somebody asked him to sing,
    Replied: "It is odd,
    But I cannot tell *God*
Save the Weasel from *Pop Goes the King*."

Anon

Song Sung by a Man on a Barge to another Man on a Different Barge in Order to Drive Him Mad

I am the best..

Oh,

I am the best bargee bar none,
You are the best bargee bar one!
You are the second-best bargee,
You are the best bargee bar me!

Oh,

I am the best . . .

(and so on, until he is
hurled into the canal)

Kit Wright

Tongue Twister

A canner exceedingly canny
One morning remarked to his granny
"A canner can can
Anything that he can,
But a canner can't can a can, can he?"

Carolyn Wells

Mr Lott's Allotment

Mr Lott's allotment
Meant a lot to Mr Lott.
Now Mr Lott is missed a lot
On Mr Lott's allotment.

Colin West

The Wizard Said:

"You find a sheltered spot that faces south. . . "
  "And then?"
"You sniff and put two fingers in your mouth . . . "
  "And then?"
"You close your eyes and roll your eye-balls round . . . "
  "And then?"
"You lift your left foot slowly off the ground . . . "
  "And then?"
"You make your palm into a kind of cup . . . "
  "And then?"
"You *very quickly* raise your right foot up . . . "
  "And then?"
"You fall over."

Richard Edwards

Its Fangs Were Red

Its fangs were red with bloody gore,
its eyes were red with menace,
it battered down my bedroom door,
and burst across my bedroom floor,
and with a loud, resounding roar
said, "ANYONE FOR TENNIS?"

Jack Prelutsky

Hurk

I'd rather play tennis than go to the dentist.
I'd rather play soccer than go to the doctor.
I'd rather play Hurk than go to work.
Hurk? Hurk? What's Hurk?
I don't know, but it *must* be better than work.

Shel Silverstein

Schoolitis

You haven't got a cough,
You haven't got mumps,
You haven't got a chill
Or any funny lumps.
You haven't got a tummy-ache,
You haven't got a fever,
You haven't got a runny nose
Or chicken-pox either.
You don't look a ruin,
You don't look a wreck,
You haven't got toothache
Or a pain in the neck.
You're fit as a fiddle,
You're sound as a bell,
In fact I've never ever
Seen you looking so well!
You don't fool me,
I'm no fool.
Now up out of bed
AND OFF TO SCHOOL!

Brian Patten

Late

You're late, said miss.
The bell has gone,
dinner numbers done
and work begun.

What have you got to say for yourself?

Well, it's like this, miss.
Me mum was sick,
me dad fell down the stairs,
the wheel fell off me bike
and then we lost our Billy's snake
behind the kitchen chairs. Earache
struck down me grampy, me gran
took quite a funny turn.
Then on the way I met this man
whose dog attacked me shin –
look, miss, you can see the blood,
it doesn't look too good,
does it?

Yes, yes, sit down –
and next time say you're sorry
for disturbing all the class.
Now, get on with your story,
fast!

Please miss, I've got nothing to write about.

Judith Nicholls

Eeyore's Poem

Christopher Robin is going.
At least I think he is.
Where?
Nobody knows.
But he is going –
I mean he goes
(*To rhyme with "knows"*)
Do we care?
(*To rhyme with "where"*)
We do
Very much.
(*I haven't got a rhyme for that
   "is" in the second line yet.*
Bother.)
(Now I haven't got a rhyme for
   bother. Bother.)
Those two bothers will have
   to rhyme with each other
Buther.
The fact is this is more difficult
   than I thought,
I ought –
(*Very good indeed*)
I ought
To begin again,
But it is easier
To stop.

Christopher Robin, good-bye,
I
(*Good*)
I
And all your friends
Sends –
I mean all your friend
Send –

(*Very awkward this, it keeps
 going wrong.*)
Well, anyhow, we send
Our love
END.

"If anybody wants to clap," said Eeyore when
he had read this, "now is the time to do it."

A. A. Milne

An Attempt at Unrhymed Verse

People tell you all the time,
Poems do not have to rhyme.
It's often better if they don't
And I'm determined this one won't.
                          Oh dear.
Never mind, I'll start again,
Busy, busy with my pen . . . cil.
I can do it, if I try —
Easy, peasy, pudding and gherkins.

Writing verse is so much fun,
Cheering as the summer weather,
Makes you feel alert and bright,
'Specially when you get it more or less the way you want it.

Wendy Cope

New Leaf

C.R.

M.V.

Today is the first day of my new book.
I've written the date
and underlined it
in red felt-tip
with a ruler.
I'm going to be different
with this book.
With this book
I'm going to be good.
With this book

I'm always going to do the date like that
dead neat
with a ruler
just like Christine Robinson.

With this book
I'll be as clever as Graham Holden,
get all my sums right, be as
neat as Mark Veitch;
I'll keep my pens and pencils
in a pencil case
and never have to borrow again.

DOG
OUR dOG

Graham Holden
is a swot

58

Miss

With this book
I'm going to work hard,
not talk, be different –
with this book,
not yell out, mess about,
be silly –
with this book.

With this book
I'll be grown-up, sensible,
and every one will want me;
I'll be picked out first
like Iain Cartwright:
no one will ever laugh at me again.
Everything will be
different

with this book . . .

Mick Gowar

← P.E. teacher

What Is This Here?

With my hands on my head, what is this here?
This is my THINKER, right over here.
That's what I learned in school.

With my hands on my head, what is this here?
This is my I-SEE-YOU, right over here.
Thinker, I-see-you, hinky dinky do.
That's what I learned in school.

With my hands on my head, what is this here?
This is my SNEEZE-MAKER, right over here.
Thinker, I-see-you, sneeze-maker, hinky dinky do.
That's what I learned in school.

With my hands on my head, what is this here?
This is my SOUP STRAINER, right over here.
Thinker, I-see-you, sneeze-maker, soup strainer,
  hinky dinky do.
That's what I learned in school.

With my hands on my neck, what is this here?
This is my COLLAR HOLDER, right over here.
Thinker, I-see-you, sneeze-maker, soup strainer,
  collar holder, hinky dinky do.
That's what I learned in school.

With my hands on my body, what is this here?
This is my BREAD BASKET, right over here.
Thinker, I-see-you, sneeze-maker, soup strainer,
    collar holder, bread basket, hinky dinky do.
That's what I learned in school.

With my hands on my body, what is this here?
This is my BELT HOLDER, right over here.
Thinker, I-see-you, sneeze-maker, soup strainer,
    collar holder, bread basket, belt holder,
    hinky dinky do.
That's what I learned in school.

With my hands on my legs, what is this here?
This is my KNEE CAPPER, right over here.
Thinker, I-see-you, sneeze-maker, soup strainer,
    collar holder, bread basket, belt holder, knee
    capper, hinky dinky do.
That's what I learned in school.

With my hands on my feet, what is this here?
This is my SHOE HOLDER, right over here.
Thinker, I-see-you, sneeze-maker, soup strainer,
    collar holder, bread basket, belt holder, knee
    capper, shoe holder, hinky dinky do.
That's what I learned in school.

Anon

The Head's Hideout

The Head crouched in his hideout
Beneath a dustbin lid.
"I want to see," he muttered,
"No teacher and no kid,

"No parent, no inspector,
Never a district nurse,
And, please, not one school dinner:
The things are getting worse!"

All morning, as the phone rang,
He hid away. Instead:
"The Head is in the dustbin,"
The secretary said.

"The *Head* is in the *dustbin*?"
"Yes, he'll be there all day.
He likes sometimes to manage
A little getaway.

"Last year he went to Holland.
Next year he's off to France.
Today he's in the dustbin.
You have to take your chance."

The Head sprang from the garbage
As end-of-school came round.
He cried, "That's quite the nastiest
Hideaway I've found!

"I think I'll stick to teachers
And kids and parents too.
It's just sometimes I've had enough."
Don't blame him. Do you?

Kit Wright

What the Headteacher Said When He Saw Me Running Out of School at 1.15 p.m. on 21 July Last Year to Buy an Ice Cream from Pellozzi's Van

HEY!*

*This poem is an attempt on three world records at once: the longest title, the longest footnote, and the shortest text of any poem in the western world. It has been lodged with *The Guinness Book of Records*.

Fred Sedgwick

Banananananananana

I thought I'd win the spelling bee
    And get right to the top,
But I started to spell "banana",
    And I didn't know when to stop.

William Cole

Hey Diddle, Diddle

Hey diddle, diddle,
The cat and the fiddle,
The cow jumped over the moon;
The little dog laughed
To see such fun,
And the dish ran away with the chocolate biscuits.

Michael Rosen

Little Miss Muffet Sat on a Tuffet

Little Miss Muffet sat on a tuffet,
Eating her curds and whey.
Along came a spider who sat down beside her
And said, "Whatcha got in the bowl, sweetheart?"

Anon

Twinkle, Twinkle Little Bat

Twinkle, twinkle, little bat!
How I wonder what you're at!
Up above the world you fly,
Like a tea-tray in the sky.
          Twinkle, twinkle . . .

Lewis Carroll

Good King Wenceslas

Good King Wenceslas walked out
    In his mother's garden.
He bumped into a Brussels sprout
    And said "I beg your pardon."

Anon

65

Thirty Days Hath September

Thirty days hath September,
And the rest I can't remember.

Michael Rosen

It's Winter, It's Winter

It's winter, it's winter, it's wonderful winter,
When everyone lounges around in the sun!

It's winter, it's winter, it's wonderful winter,
When everyone's brown like a steak overdone!

It's winter, it's winter, it's wonderful winter,
It's swimming and surfing and hunting for conkers!

It's winter, it's winter, it's wonderful winter,
And I am completely and utterly bonkers!

66   *Kit Wright*

Frost on the Flower

Frost on the flower,
Leaf and frond,
Snow on the field-path,
Ice on the pond.

Out of the east
A white wind comes.
Hail on the rooftop
Kettledrums.

Snow-fog wanders
Hollow and hill.
Along the valley
The stream is still.

Thunder and lightning.
Down slaps the rain.
No doubt about it.
Summer again.

Charles Causley

August

The sprinkler twirls.
    The summer wanes.
The pavement wears
    Popsicle stains.

The playground grass
    Is worn to dust.
The weary swings
    Creak, creak with rust.

The trees are bored
    With being green.
Some people leave
    The local scene

And go to seaside
    Bungalows
And take off nearly
    All their clothes.

John Updike

Whether the Weather

Whether the weather be fine
Or whether the weather be not
Whether the weather be cold
Or whether the weather be hot –
We'll weather the weather
Whatever the weather
Whether we like it or not!

Anon

The Sunlight Falls Upon the Grass

The sunlight falls upon the grass;
It falls upon the tower;
Upon my spectacles of brass
It falls with all its power.

It falls on everything it can,
For that is how it's made;
And it would fall on me, except,
That I am in the shade.

Mervyn Peake

'Twas in the Month of Liverpool

'Twas in the month of Liverpool
In the city of July,
The snow was raining heavily,
The streets were very dry.
The flowers were sweetly singing,
The birds were in full bloom,
As I went down the cellar
To sweep an upstairs room.

Anon

The Rain

The rain it raineth on the just
And also on the unjust fella.
But chiefly on the just, because
The unjust steals the just's umbrella.

Baron Charles Bowen

The Storm Starts

The storm starts
when the drops start dropping.
When the drops stop dropping
then the storm starts stopping.

Dr Seuss

Mud

I like mud.
     I like it on my clothes.
I like it on my fingers.
     I like it on my toes.

Dirt's pretty ordinary
     And dust's a dud.
For a really good mess-up
     I like mud.

John Smith

The Mississippi

I am Old Man Mississippi,
full of Time and Mud –
you all must be pretty nippy
if I ever flood!
Swim in me? You would be dippy!
Foolish flesh and blood
would end woeful, dead and drippy!
Keep your distance, bud!

Gavin Ewart

Went to the River

Went to the river, couldn't get across,
Paid five dollars for an old gray hoss.
Hoss wouldn't pull so I traded for a bull.
Bull wouldn't holler so I traded for a dollar.
Dollar wouldn't pass so I threw it on the grass.
Grass wouldn't grow so I traded for a hoe.
Hoe wouldn't dig so I traded for a pig.
Pig wouldn't squeal so I traded for a wheel.
Wheel wouldn't run so I traded for a gun.
Gun wouldn't shoot so I traded for a boot.
Boot wouldn't fit so I thought I'd better quit.
So I quit.

Anon

Daddy Fell into the Pond

Everyone grumbled. The sky was grey.
We had nothing to do and nothing to say.
We were nearing the end of a dismal day.
And there seemed to be nothing beyond,
   Then
     Daddy fell into the pond!

And everyone's face grew merry and bright,
And Timothy danced for sheer delight.
"Give me the camera, quick, oh quick!
He's crawling out of the duckweed!" Click!

Then the gardener suddenly slapped his knee,
And doubled up, shaking silently,
And the ducks all quacked as if they were daft,
And it sounded as if the old drake laughed.
Oh, there wasn't a thing that didn't respond
   When
     Daddy fell into the pond!

Alfred Noyes

72

The Train to Glasgow

Here is the train to Glasgow.

Here is the driver,
Mr MacIver,
Who drove the train to Glasgow.

Here is the guard from Donibristle
Who waved his flag and blew his whistle
To tell the driver,
Mr MacIver,
To start the train to Glasgow.

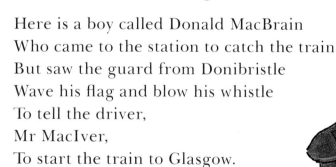

Here is a boy called Donald MacBrain
Who came to the station to catch the train
But saw the guard from Donibristle
Wave his flag and blow his whistle
To tell the driver,
Mr MacIver,
To start the train to Glasgow.

Here is the guard, a kindly man
Who, at the last moment, hauled into the van
That fortunate boy called Donald MacBrain
Who came to the station to catch the train
But saw the guard from Donibristle
Wave his flag and blow his whistle
To tell the driver,
Mr MacIver,
To start the train to Glasgow.

Here are hens and here are cocks,
Clucking and crowing inside a box,
In charge of the guard, that kindly man
Who, at the last moment, hauled into the van
That fortunate boy called Donald MacBrain
Who came to the station to catch the train
But saw the guard from Donibristle
Wave his flag and blow his whistle
To tell the driver,
Mr MacIver,
To start the train to Glasgow.

Here is the train. It gave a jolt
Which loosened a catch and loosened a bolt,
And let out the hens and let out the cocks,
Clucking and crowing out of their box,
In charge of the guard, that kindly man
Who, at the last moment, hauled into the van
That fortunate boy called Donald MacBrain
Who came to the station to catch the train
But saw the guard from Donibristle
Wave his flag and blow his whistle.
To tell the driver,
Mr MacIver,
To start the train to Glasgow.

The guard chased a hen and, missing it, fell.
The hens were all squawking, the cocks were as well,
And unless you were there you haven't a notion
The flurry, the fuss, the noise and commotion
Caused by the train which gave a jolt
And loosened a catch and loosened a bolt
And let out the hens and let out the cocks,
Clucking and crowing out of their box,
In charge of the guard, that kindly man
Who, at the last moment, hauled into the van
That fortunate boy called Donald MacBrain
Who came to the station to catch the train
But saw the guard from Donibristle
Wave his flag and blow his whistle
To tell the driver,
Mr MacIver,
To start the train to Glasgow.

Now Donald was quick and Donald was neat
And Donald was nimble on his feet.
He caught the hens and he caught the cocks
And he put them back in their great big box.
The guard was pleased as pleased could be
And invited Donald to come to tea
On Saturday, at Donibristle,
And let him blow his lovely whistle,
And said in all his life he'd never
Seen a boy so quick and clever,
And so did the driver,
Mr MacIver,
Who drove the train to Glasgow.

Wilma Horsbrugh

Let Basil Go to Basildon

Let Basil go to Basildon,
Let Lester go to Leicester;
Let Steven go to Stevenage
With raincoat and sou'wester.

Let Peter go to Peterhead,
Let Dudley go to Dudley;
Let Milton go to Milton Keynes –
The pavements there are puddly.

Let Felix go to Felixstowe,
Let Barry go to Barry;
Let Mabel go to Mablethorpe,
But I at home shall tarry.

Let Alice go to Alice Springs,
Let Florence go to Florence;
Let Benny go to Benidorm
Where rain comes down in torrents.

Let Winnie go to Winnipeg,
Let Sidney go to Sydney;
Let Otto go to Ottawa –
I am not of that kidney.

Let Vera go to Veracruz,
Let Nancy go to Nancy,
But I'll stay home while others roam –
Abroad I do not fancy.

Colin West

Morning, Mrs McCave, letter for Dave...

Too Many Daves

Did I ever tell you that Mrs McCave
Had twenty-three sons and she named them all Dave?
Well, she did. And that wasn't a smart thing to do.
You see, when she wants one and calls out, "Yoo-Hoo!
Come into the house, Dave!" she doesn't get *one*.
All twenty-three Daves of hers come on the run!
This makes things quite difficult at the McCaves'
As you can imagine, with so many Daves.
And often she wishes that, when they were born,
She had named one of them Bodkin Van Horn
And one of them Hoos-Foos. And one of them Snimm.
And one of them Hot-Shot. And one Sunny Jim.
And one of them Shadrack. And one of them Blinkey.
And one of them Stuffy. And one of them Stinkey.
Another one Putt-Putt. Another one Moon Face.
Another one Marvin O'Gravel Balloon Face.
And one of them Ziggy. And one Soggy Muff.
One Buffalo Bill. And one Biffalo Buff.
And one of them Sneepy. And one Weepy Weed.
And one Paris Garters. And one Harris Tweed.
And one of them Sir Michael Carmichael Zutt
And one of them Oliver Boliver Butt
And one of them Zanzibar Buck-Buck McFate . . .
But she didn't do it. And now it's too late.

Dr Seuss

Acknowledgements

'I Din Do Nuttin' by John Agard from I DIN DO NUTTIN, published by Hutchinson and reprinted by permission of The Random Century Group; 'The Dobermann Dog' by George Barker from RUNES AND RHYMES AND TUNES AND CHIMES, published by and reprinted by permission of Faber and Faber Limited; 'Mr Skinner' by N M Bodecker from LET'S MARRY SAID THE CHERRY, published by and reprinted by permission of Faber and Faber Limited; 'Frost on the Flower' by Charles Causley from THE YOUNG MAN OF CURY, published by Macmillan and reprinted by permission of David Higham Associates; 'There Was an Old Woman' by Charles Causley from EARLY IN THE MORNING, published by Macmillan and reprinted by permission of David Higham Associates; 'Banananananananana' © 1977 William Cole; 'An Attempt at Unrhymed Verse' © Wendy Cope, reprinted by permission of the author; 'Telling' by Wendy Cope from TWIDDLING YOUR THUMBS, published by and reprinted by permission of Faber and Faber Limited; 'L' by Sue Cowling from WHAT IS A KUMQUAT?, published by and reprinted by permission of Faber and Faber Limited; 'The Song of a Mole' by Richard Edwards from THE WORD PARTY, published by Lutterworth Press 1986; 'The Wizard Said' by Richard Edwards from WHISPERS FROM A WARDROBE, published by Lutterworth Press 1987; 'The Mississippi' by Gavin Ewart from THE COLLECTED EWART 1980 – 1990, published by Hutchinson; 'Literalist' © John Fandel; 'New Leaf' by Mick Gowar from THIRD TIME LUCKY © Mick Gowar 1988, published by Viking Kestrel, 1988; 'Sometime the Cow Kick Your Head' © Andrew J. Grossman; 'Brother' by Mary Ann Hobermann from HELLO AND GOODBY, (1959), published by Little Brown and Co and reprinted by permission of Gina Maccoby Literary Agency; 'Chips' © Julie Holder from A VERY FIRST POETRY BOOK, published by Oxford University Press; 'The Train to Glasgow' by Wilma Horsbrugh from CLINKERDUMP, published by Methuen Children's Books and reprinted by permission of Reed Book Services; 'Giraffes Don't Huff' by Karla Kuskin from ROAR AND MORE, published by Harper and Row and reprinted by permission of HarperCollins; 'Puddin' Song' by Norman Lindsay from THE MAGIC PUDDING © Jane Glad 1918, and reprinted by permission of Angus and Robertson Publishers; 'Easy Money' and 'The Leader' by Roger McGough from A PIE IN THE SKY published by Puffin Books, and reprinted by permission of the Peters, Fraser and Dunlop Group; 'Three Riddled Riddles' © Ian McMillan and Martyn Wiley; 'Monday's Child is Red and Spotty' and 'The Human Siren' by Colin McNaughton from THERE'S AN AWFUL LOT OF WEIRDOS IN OUR NEIGHBOURHOOD © 1987 Colin McNaughton, published in the UK by Walker Books Limited; 'Mum is Having a Baby' by Colin McNaughton from WHO'S BEEN SLEEPING IN MY PORRIDGE? © Colin McNaughton, published in the UK by Walker Books Limited; 'Bad Sir Brian Botany' by A.A. Milne from WHEN WE WERE VERY YOUNG, published by Methuen Children's Books and reprinted by permission of Reed Book Services; 'Cottleston Pie' by A.A. Milne from WINNIE THE POOH, published by Methuen Children's Books and reprinted by permission of Reed Book Services; 'Eeyore's Poem' by A.A. Milne from THE HOUSE AT POOH CORNER, published by Methuen Children's Books and reprinted by permission of Reed Book Services; 'The Tree Frog' by John Travers Moore from CINNAMON SEED, copyright © 1967 John Travers Moore, and published by Houghton Mifflin Co.; 'Adventures of Isabel' by Ogden Nash from ADVENTURES OF ISABEL, published by and reprinted by permission of Little Brown and Company; 'My Cousin Melda' © Grace Nichols; 'Late' by Judith Nicholls from MAGIC MIRROR, published by and reprinted by permission of Faber and Faber Limited; 'Schoolitis' by Brian Patten from THAWING FROZEN FROGS, published by Viking and reprinted by permission of Rogers, Coleridge and White Ltd; 'The Sunlight Falls Upon the Grass' by Mervyn Peake, from RHYMES WITHOUT REASON, published by Methuen and reprinted by permission of David Higham Associates; 'I'm in a Rotten Mood' and 'Its Fangs Were Red' by Jack Prelutsky from NEW KID ON THE BLOCK, published by William Heinemann and reprinted by permission of Reed Book Services; 'My Brother's on the Floor Roaring' by Michael Rosen from WHO DREW ON THE BABY'S HEAD? published by Andre Deutsch and reprinted by permission of Scholastic Publications Ltd; 'Hey, Diddle, Diddle' and 'Thirty Days Hath September' by Michael Rosen from HAIRY TALES AND NURSERY CRIMES, published by Andre Deutsch and reprinted by permission of Scholastic Publications Ltd; 'Why Did the Children' by Carl Sandburg from THE PEOPLE, YES, published by and reprinted by permission of Harcourt, Brace and Company; excerpt from 'Oh Can You Say' © 1979 by Dr Seuss and A. S. Geisel, published by HarperCollins and reprinted by permission of Elaine Greene Ltd; 'Too Many Daves' by Dr Seuss from THE SNEETCHES AND OTHER STORIES published by HarperCollins and reprinted by permission of Elaine Greene Ltd; 'What the Headteacher Said When He Saw Me. . .' by Fred Sedgwick from HEY! © Mary Glasgow Publications Ltd, London; 'Friendship' and 'Hurk' from A LIGHT IN THE ATTIC by Shel Silverstein. Copyright © 1981 by Evil Eye Music, Inc. By permission of Edite Kroll Literary Agency; 'Mud' by John Smith, published by Harrap and reprinted by permission of Chambers Publishers; 'The Burglar' and 'Into the Mixer' by Matthew Sweeney from THE FLYING SPRING ONION, published by and reprinted by permission of Faber and Faber Limited; 'August' by John Updike from A CHILD'S CALENDAR, published by Random House and reprinted by permission of Scholastic Publications Ltd; 'Here is the Nose That Smelled Something Sweet' by Clyde Watson from CATCH ME AND KISS ME AND SAY IT AGAIN, published by HarperCollins and reprinted by permission of Curtis Brown Associates Ltd; 'Christine Crump' © Colin West from IT'S FUNNY WHEN YOU LOOK AT IT; 'Let Basil go to Basildon' and 'Mr Lott's Allotment' by Colin West from WHAT WOULD YOU DO WITH A WOBBLE-DE-WOO? published by Hutchinson and reprinted by permission of The Random Century Group; 'The Head's Hideout' by Kit Wright from CAT AMONG THE PIGEONS, copyright © Kit Wright, 1984, 1987. Published by Viking Kestrel, 1987; 'If You're No Good at Cooking' by Kit Wright, from RABBITING ON, published by and reprinted by permission of Lions, an imprint of HarperCollins Publishers Ltd; 'It's Winter, It's Winter' by Kit Wright from HOT DOG, copyright © Kit Wright 1981. Published by Viking Kestrel Books, 1981; 'Song Sung by a Man on a Barge to Another Man on a Different Barge in Order to Drive Him Mad' by Kit Wright from HOT DOG, copyright © Kit Wright, 1981. Published by Viking Kestrel Books, 1981.

Index of authors and first lines

For Sally

A.F.

Poor Monty

ANNE FINE
Illustrated by Clara Vulliamy

MAMMOTH

Monty's mother was a doctor.

A very busy doctor.

She spent her mornings at the surgery.

She spent her lunch times driving
round seeing the old folk.

And she spent her afternoons filling in forms.

By the time she came home, all she wanted was to put her feet up and have a cup of tea and a quiet little read of the paper.

Monty tried talking to her.
"*Suppose*," he said, "suppose you felt
funny all over and a little bit shivery . . ."

"Mmmm," said his mother, turning over a page.

"And *suppose*," said Monty,
"suppose your forehead was hot . . .

And suppose your head felt as if
little men in steel boots were stamping in it . . ."

"And suppose your tummy felt as
if people had made you eat worms . . ."

"Mmmmm," said his mother, turning another page.

"And suppose," bellowed Monty,
"suppose when you lifted up
your shirt you found you had
little red spots all over your body!"

And he burst into tears.

Monty's mother scooped him
up and cuddled him.
"Oh, poor Monty!" she said.
"What a terrible doctor I am!
You've got chicken-pox!"

And Monty felt a little better already.

First published in Great Britain 1992
by Methuen Children's Books Ltd
Published 1996 by Mammoth
an imprint of Reed International Books Ltd
Michelin House, 81 Fulham Road, London SW3 6RB
and Auckland, Melbourne, Singapore and Toronto

ISBN 0 7497 2749 7

A CIP catalogue record for this title
is available from the British Library

Produced by Mandarin Offset Ltd
Printed and bound in China

10 9 8 7 6 5 4 3 2

Honeysuckle Cottage
Poppy's House

Forget-Me-Not Cottage
Grandpa's House and Office

Poppy Field

Honeypot Cottage
...ney and Granny Bumble's House

Blossom
Bakehouse

Cornsilk Castle
and Courtyard

Village Hall

Sage's
Vet Surgery

Post Office

River Swan

Beehive
Beauty Salon

Barley Farm
The Meadowsweets' House

Riverside
Stables

Honeypot Hill
Railway Station

To Camomile Cove
via Periwinkle Lane

N
W   E
S

Check out Princess Poppy's brilliant website:

www.princesspoppy.com

MERMAID PRINCESS
A PICTURE CORGI BOOK 978 0 552 56310 9

First published in Great Britain by Picture Corgi,
an imprint of Random House Children's Books
A Random House Group Company

This edition published 2009

3 5 7 9 10 8 6 4 2

Text copyright © Janey Louise Jones, 2009
Illustration copyright © Picture Corgi Books, 2009
Illustrations by Veronica Vasylenko
Design by Tracey Cunnell

The right of Janey Louise Jones to be identified as the author of this work has been
asserted in accordance with the Copyright, Designs and Patents Act 1988.

Picture Corgi Books are published by Random House Children's Books,
61–63 Uxbridge Road, London W5 5SA

www.kidsatrandomhouse.co.uk
www.princesspoppy.com

Addresses for companies within The Random House Group Limited
can be found at: www.randomhouse.co.uk/offices.htm

THE RANDOM HOUSE GROUP Limited Reg. No. 954009

A CIP catalogue record for this book is available from the British Library.

Printed in China

Mermaid Princess

Written by Janey Louise Jones

PICTURE CORGI

For Evelyn, Julie and Lilian,
my special friends,
with love

★

Mermaid Princess

featuring

Honey
★

Daisy
★

Edward
★

Princess Poppy

Flora
★

Mum
★

Dad
★

"Hurrah! I love carnival day!" Poppy cried as the train chuffed into Camomile Cove station.

"Me too!" replied Honey. "I really hope one of us will be crowned Mermaid Princess this year!"

As soon as the train stopped at the platform, Poppy and Honey jumped down and started making their way towards Shellbay House, where Poppy's cousin, Daisy lived.

They couldn't wait to put on their carnival costumes and join the parade.

"Hang on, girls," called Mum as the grown-ups tried to organize the twins and all the picnic baskets and buckets and spades, but Poppy and Honey were already halfway up the road.

"Hi, Daisy!" said Poppy as they saw her older cousin waving from the doorway of her summer house. "Wow! Your costume is amazing."

Daisy was already dressed up in her mermaid outfit, all ready for the carnival, so she helped the other two girls to get changed into theirs.

Then she styled their hair
and added a few accessories.

"I'm sure one of you two will win the Mermaid Princess crown this year!" exclaimed Daisy when Poppy and Honey's outfits were complete.

They were sparkling with sequins, beads and pearly shells and they both looked wonderful.

Just then Daisy's younger brother, Edward, burst through the door.

"Come on, you lot. We have to leave for the parade, or Mum says we'll all be late," he said.

The happy group hurried to the clock tower, where the children's parade was about to begin. Poppy, Honey, Daisy and Edward waved goodbye to the grown-ups and the twins and set off round the town with all the other children.

The parade was amazing to look at with so many wonderful costumes – although Poppy secretly thought hers was the best – and lots of brightly coloured streamers and balloons. They were so excited to be part of it.

Just then, among all the noise and people, Poppy noticed a girl standing all alone.

"Are you all right?" called Poppy as she pushed through the parade towards her.

"No!" sobbed the little girl miserably. "My tiara has been knocked off and now it's broken so my costume is spoiled *and* I've lost my friends."

"Oh, poor you!" said Poppy. "I'm Poppy. What's your name?"

"It's Flora Jane Tomkins," replied the girl, between sniffs and sobs.

"Why don't you come with me and my friends?" suggested Poppy.
"We'll help you find your friends after the parade."

"Yes please," replied Flora, smiling through her tears.

Then Poppy did something very unusual . . .

"Oh, and why don't you have this?" said Poppy, taking off her tiara and offering it to Flora. "I've got so many sparkly things on my costume that I don't really need it anyway."

"Are you sure?" asked Flora as she took the tiara and put it on.

"Um, yes," said Poppy, pleased that she had made Flora feel better but a little sad about giving away her gorgeous tiara.

"Thank you!" smiled Flora.

"Come on, Poppy!" called Daisy, suddenly noticing that her cousin had dropped behind. "The costume competition is in five minutes."

"Coming," replied Poppy as she grabbed Flora's hand and made her way towards the others.

As the parade came to a stop, Daisy looked at Poppy's bare head, then at Flora's tiara, but before she could ask what had happened, an announcement started booming through the loud speakers.

"To find out who will be crowned this year's Mermaid Princess and Lord of the Sea, can all those contestants wishing to take part in the costume competition please make their way to the harbour wall immediately?"

Poppy, Daisy, Honey, Edward and Flora stood by the harbour wall together, all dizzy with nerves and excitement. Each of them was absolutely desperate to win!

The boy's prize was announced first and the girls went wild when
Edward's name was called. They giggled as he hopped onto the platform
on one leg and was crowned Lord of the Sea.

All the mermaids in the crowd began to tremble as the special coral crown of the Mermaid Princess was taken from the prize box. Poppy held her breath.

"This year, we are awarding the Mermaid Princess prize to a very special girl. She has a wonderful costume but there was something else we noticed during the parade, something more important than her costume.

She knows what I'm talking about. So I am delighted to announce that this year, the Mermaid Princess prize goes to . . .

"Miss Poppy Cotton. Come up to the stage please, Princess Poppy!"
Poppy felt as if she was dreaming. Daisy proudly led her onto
the stage. Mum waved up at her, while Dad took photographs.

Poppy smiled as the judge put the magnificent coral crown on her head.

"Now, to complete the carnival parade the Mermaid Princess and the Lord of the Sea will ride through the streets in a horse-drawn carriage," said the judge as the crowd clapped and cheered.

All of Poppy's friends and family, including Flora, who had now been reunited with her own group, followed the carriage, cheering all the way. Dad jogged to keep up so that he could take photos.

"You're a perfect Mermaid Princess, Poppy," said Dad when the carriage came to a stop. "The kindest princess — which is why you deserve your coral crown!"

Poppy smiled — it had been the best carnival ever!